OLD TESTAMENT PRAYER
Faith of Our Fathers

Stephen Eyre

VICTOR BOOKS

A DIVISION OF SCRIPTURE PRESS PUBLICATIONS INC.
USA   CANADA   ENGLAND

Scripture quotations are from the *Holy Bible, New International Version*®. Copyright © 1973, 1978, 1984 by International Bible Society. Used by permission of Zondervan Publishing House. All rights reserved.

The story in the introduction is adapted from "George and the Dragon," from *The Furniture of Heaven* by Mike Mason, © 1989. Used by permission of Harold Shaw Publishers, Wheaton, IL.

Editor: Carolyn Nystrom
Designer: Scott Rattray
Cover Photo: Charles Gupton

Recommended Dewey Decimal Classification: 248.3
Suggested Subject Heading: PERSONAL RELIGION: PRAYER
ISBN: 1-56476-368-4

1 2 3 4 5 6 7 8 9 10 Printing/Year 99 98 97 96 95

Copyright © 1995 by Victor Books/SP Publications, Inc. All rights reserved. Printed in the United States of America.

No part of this book may be reproduced without written permission, except for brief quotations in books and critical reviews. For information write Victor Books, 1825 College Avenue, Wheaton, Illinois 60187.

Contents

Welcome to TruthSeed

I am a planter. Each spring finds me stooped in my garden, loose dirt churned soft by winter storms oozing into my worn sneakers, the smell of compost twitching my nose, warm sun thawing the muscles of my back, and precious seed—radish, carrots, lettuce, peas, beans, corn, beets, watermelon, cantaloupe, squash, cosmos, marigold, zinnia—trickling through my fingers. It's my favorite phase of gardening, one I try to remember as I tug at thick weeds in late June's humidity, swat mosquitoes in sweltering July twilight, and heft baskets of produce into my August-cluttered kitchen. I cut, peel, blanch, can, freeze, and (in recent years) mostly give away—with neighbors and coworkers cashing in on my penchant for planting. It's hard to believe that seeds barely filling a lunch bag spend a few weeks blending God's creative magic of sun, soil, and water into a winter's worth of food for a family. But that's what seed is all about. Abundant life encased in a tiny, hard shell.

No mere book can deliver full-grown, harvested produce—though some come close. Like seeds, books contain a grain of truth encased in the crusty shell of words. But plant that seed in the right season in a mind ready to learn, tug out the weeds of distraction that disrupt study, water it with a sweated-out attempt to put its truths into practice, invite with prayer the sunshine of God's grace, and expect a crop—enough to nurture personal growth, enough to give away.

What harvest can we expect from TruthSeed?

We can expect to know Scripture. Each book in this series invites us either to explore a topic addressed in several biblical passages or to study an entire book of the Bible. These are inductive studies. Each session leads us to explore a single passage on three levels: details of information presented in the text, accurate interpretation of that information, and personal response.

We can expect to experience God's presence. Scripture points us to God, its author and its object. It is His letter to us about Himself. As we read, study, and meditate on Scripture we will become more and more aware of God. We will see His love and wrath, His mercy and justice, acted out on the pages of these ancient texts. And we will know more and more about God's personal care for us and His desire for us to respond to Him.

We can expect to improve our relationships. Human nature is remarkably resilient; over the millennia we have changed little. Scripture shows us brothers who hate each other enough to kill, and friends who love each other more than their own lives. It shows us the grief of death and the joy of birth. It shows us the celebration of marriage and the pain of marriage ended. It pictures overwhelming generosity and the grudging hunger of greed. It echoes our hopeless moans at life's futility and it shouts our hope for life beyond this life. As Scripture increases our understanding of each other, we can expect to see its fruit wherever we touch other people: at work, in friendships, at churches, in neighborhoods, in casual encounters with waitresses and store clerks, and in the most challenging of all relationships: our families.

We can expect to better understand ourselves. Scripture is an intensely personal book. True, we may read it for historical content, or for its quality literature, or for its insightful teachings. But if Scripture is to accomplish its true purpose, we must read its pages, open ourselves, and allow it to read our souls. Scripture will show us our faults: the jealous brother, the greedy servant, the pompous keeper of laws. But as we let Scripture do its work, we will grow more and more according to God's design: the forgiving parent, the faithful leader, the wise friend, the one who models the love of Jesus Christ. And we will find the empty, God-shaped hole inside being filled by Christ Himself. Even people who don't believe much of what the Bible says, who are turned off by sermons and essays, can appreciate the questions here that allow them to examine the biblical text for themselves, explore its potential meanings, and form personal conclusions about response.

TruthSeed is appropriate for small group discussion or for personal use. Its blend of academic, personal, and relational tasks make it ideal for cell groups, workplace study groups, neighborhood groups, school-based groups, Sunday School classes, retreats, and outreach groups. It is also for personal study, meditation, and growth.

Suggestions for Group Discussion

1. There's no need to be a Bible expert to participate in a TruthSeed discussion. You may find experts in your group, but there is plenty of room for non-experts as well. Since the discussion centers around a single passage, you will all participate on a similar level. And God can grow any of us.

2. Arrive on time — out of consideration for other group members. Bring your TruthSeed guide and a Bible.

3. Commit to regular attendance. Understanding of the Scripture and relationships within the group are cumulative. You and others will benefit most if you can count on each other to be there. If you must be absent, call your host or leader ahead of time.

4. Discussion is a shared responsibility. It blends talking and listening in even balance. If you are a born listener, act on your responsibility to share your insights by making the extra effort necessary. If you are a born talker, sharpen your listening skills by keeping track of the flow of conversation. If you discover that you are "on stage" more than the average person present, shorten your comments and use them to draw other people into the conversation.

5. Treat other group members with respect. You cannot possibly agree with every comment throughout the course of a discussion study. Disagreement is one way to help each other grow toward the truth. But express your disagreement in kind terms that reflect a genuine respect for the person.

6. Guard the privacy of people in your group. Since spiritual growth makes a deep impact on our personal lives, you will likely hear others speak of their private feelings and events. And you may want to speak some of your own private thoughts. Agree together that you will not divulge each other's stories.

7. Don't gossip. Many groups pray together for a variety of needy people. It's tempting to get specific about names and weaknesses in a way that invites more speculation than prayer. Don't do it. It's possible to pray for a person with very little inside information. God knows it anyway.

8. Be willing to discuss the application questions. Some people are content to keep a group study at a purely academic level, so they read the questions that invite personal response, and pass on with the quick instruction to "think about it." But if Scripture is to be more than a textbook of information, we must allow it to penetrate our lives. Members of a group can nurture each other toward spiritual growth as they discuss together its personal impact.

9. Take note of the follow-up assignments. Each TruthSeed study ends with supplementary material that can provide further enrichment. In some cases, this section may prove as valuable as the rest of the study. So take advantage of this added resource.

10. Consider leading a discussion. Many groups rotate leadership so that almost everyone takes a turn asking the questions. This job does not require a lot of special skills, but a few pointers won't hurt. If it's your turn to lead, you will find *Notes for Leaders* beginning on page 63.

Suggestions for Personal Study

1. Settle into your favorite "quiet time" spot. Bring your Bible, the TruthSeed guide, writing materials, and (if you like) a commentary or Bible dictionary.

2. Pray. Ask God to reveal Himself to you as you study. Ask that He assist your understanding, that He bare your inner self to His gaze, and that He use your time to bring healing to your relationships.

3. Begin by reading the chapter introduction. Make notes about the first question and allow it to help you approach the topic you are about to study.

4. Read the assigned biblical text. If textual accuracy is one of your priorities, use a contemporary translation (not a paraphrase) that reflects recent scholarship. Mark significant words or phrases in your Bible, draw lines between ideas that seem connected, write questions or comments in the margins. Try reading aloud. It's one of the best ways to keep your mind from wandering.

5. Work through the list of questions. Jot notes in the space provided. Keep a journal of answers that require more space or more lengthy personal reflection.

6. Stop for periods of silence and meditation throughout your quiet time to allow God to work in your inner being.

7. Continue to pray as you study, asking God to reveal what He wants you to know of yourself and of Himself. Read aloud sections of the passage as a prayer inserting "I" and "me" where appropriate — or insert the name of someone you care about.

8. Don't feel that you must do an entire lesson at a single sitting. Feel free to break at natural division points or whenever you have "had enough" for now. Then come back on a different day, reread the text, review your work thus far, and pick up where you left off.

9. When you have completed your personal study of the questions, turn to the appropriate leader's notes in the back of the guide to gain further information you may have missed. If you are the studious type, refer to a commentary or Bible dictionary for more insights. The reading list at the end of the book provides a list of reliable resources.

10. Put the follow-up activities at the end of each study into practice. Read, sing, pray, do, meditate, journal, make the phone call, start the project, repair the relationship. When your study time is finished, God's work in your life has just begun. Allow His work to continue throughout the week.

As you use this TruthSeed guide, I pray that seeds of truth from God's Word will grow a rich harvest in your life.

— Carolyn Nystrom, Editor

Introducing Old Testament Prayer

George, sitting on the green grass under a tree, was taking a much-deserved rest. Just the day before he had vanquished the dragon and saved the fair damsel. Already the fame of his deed was spreading throughout the kingdom. He hadn't been declared a saint yet, but he could already sense that such an honor was impending.

Beside him on the grass rested a large basket full of culinary delights packed by the grateful maid he had rescued. Anticipating the scones and jam, he set them aside until after he finished the large apple that had first caught his eye. Upon taking a bite of apple, he discovered a large worm. Without another thought he tossed the apple, worm and all, into the moat.

As he spread the jam on a scone, he heard a churning commotion in the water across the grassy knoll. Looking over, he saw the discarded worm swimming toward the bank. He walked over to watch more closely. It grew, first from a small, wiggly worm into a long, black eel. As the eel swam toward the shore, it continued to stretch and thicken into an ugly, black snake.

George the dragon slayer, fresh from yesterday's battle, knew how to handle such enchanted foes. He ran back to his tree, strapped on his sword, snatched up his shield, and strode forward to the battle. With the first slash of his sword, he expected to vanquish the beast. But instead of slicing through the body of the snake, George's sword struck and glanced off. Where he should have seen blood, he saw only gleaming silver scale. George struck again and again and again — each time with the same result. After each blow silver scales appeared all over the snake's body. Blow by blow they formed into a mantle of gleaming armor.

Because the sword was not working, he tried to smash the head of the snake with the steel-plated heel of his boot. With the first stomp the head seemed to spread out in a triangular fashion. He stomped again. The result was a deep impression on the beast's head. From the impression spouted two ridges of triangular shape that spread from the head down the back. He stomped one last time and the head of the snake elongated to form an ugly snout with jagged fangs.

Now George was becoming unsettled. He recalled that yesterday's battle hadn't gone like this at all. His confidence shaken, he ran back to his horse and grabbed the lance. Aiming at the one place not yet covered by the scales, he thrust his lance into the soft underbelly of the monster. His well-aimed blow struck so hard that it pierced all the way through the body and out its back. From the gash in the back it appeared that part of the monster's body was spilling out. That made George feel better—but only for a moment. What appeared to be twin bladders continued to lengthen and grow into a set of wings.

With a growing sense of anxiety, George looked around and did the only thing left to him. He ran across the drawbridge and took refuge in the castle. From behind the safety of the portcullis, he watched as the beast continued to grow until it surpassed the size of the dragon he had destroyed the day before. George took an arrow and made careful aim for the beast's eye. Just before the arrow struck, the dragon turned its head and the arrow embedded in the top of his drooling jaw. There it began to thicken and curve into a cruelly shaped horn.

Leaping into the air, the dragon flew toward the castle, up over the drawbridge, and passed through the iron grate. How was this possible? George turned and ran down the steps of the nearest corridor toward the dungeon. He could hear the roar of the dragon close behind. He seized a burning torch on the wall and threw it behind him. He turned to look as the dragon opened his mouth and swallowed the burning missile. The dragon gave a roar, belched out a scorching flame, rose in the air and vanished!

Far from feeling free and relieved at the disappearance of his foe,

George began to tremble. He could feel the presence of the monster's flame as it surged through his veins. Knowing that the foe was closer than his skin, knowing too that his foe was the construction of his own prideful arrogance, George did the only thing left to him. He fell to his knees and prayed. At that point he moved from being just another chivalrous knight in search of a quest to the man later known as Saint George, the patron saint of England.

Facing Our Own Dragon

At some point in our lives in the fullness of God's time, we come to understand that the real battles we face are spiritual, that the battleground is within our souls, and that the foes we face are empowered by our own arrogance. When that happens (if we are wise) we do the only thing left to us: we pray.

We must pray. It is our only hope. Spiritual warriors of today, however, face an additional problem: we are children of a spiritually darkened age. (Not that any age of history was especially bright.) But we face an added problem. We live in a culture that has institutionalized spiritual blindness. God has been exiled to the edges of our society. Government, education, recreation—all areas of our society are conducted and constructed without reference to God. Reduced to a one-dimensional reality, it is hard for us to believe that anything beyond our five senses actually exists. Heaven, hell, God, the soul, prayer—these things aren't tangible. So we doubt that they are real—even if we are determined to believe they are.

But no matter how great the obstacles we face, the task we face is to pray. Once we do pray, we begin to discover that the battles within can be faced by the power of divine resources beyond our own. And once we face the inner battles we can begin to turn outward to a world that needs to be wrestled back into relationship with its Creator.

Learning to Pray

When we know so little of the spiritual dimensions of reality, how is it possible to know that what we say as we speak our desires heavenward is really prayer—really communication with our Creator? Jesus gave His disciples the key to prayer; we are to pray in His name. But what does that mean? Certainly it means more than the liturgical formula "in Jesus' name" that we attach at the end of our petitions. To understand Jesus' instructions on prayer, we must see them against the background of the Old Testament. So in this guide on prayer I invite you and your friends to explore six prayers of people who knew how to pray.

Abraham knew how to pray. Not because he was especially pious, but because God taught him. He learned over the pilgrimage of life that God could be counted on. He learned to offer prayers with a courageous, even audacious faith. In the excerpt of his life that we study, Abraham wants to know why God hasn't kept His promise of a son. When God reaffirms His promise Abraham says, "How can I know for sure?" God responds by the offer of a covenant-promise. That promise then became the foundation of all other prayers to follow.

Moses knew how to pray. He too expected God to keep up His end of a bargain. After the episode with the golden calf and the broken law, Moses wants God to know that trying to lead these Israelite people is a lousy, soul-crushing job. In prayer Moses asks what God is going to do about helping him. Instead of thunder-and-lightning judgment, Moses gets what amounts to an affectionate, caressing revelation of God's character.

David was a man who knew how to pray and get answers. We will look at a Psalm in which he exalts, "I sought the LORD and He answered me." We will also explore a prayer of consecration in which David seeks to tie God and his son Solomon to a massive building campaign. Just as Abraham wanted a promise from God for the birth of a son, so David seeks a promise from God in the construction of the temple.

Solomon, the son of David, knew how to pray in a way that pleased God. At one point, God was so pleased with Solomon's prayers that God gave him a secret desire that Solomon had never even voiced. In the prayer of Solomon that you study, you will see that he understood all about a God who makes and keeps His promises. Solomon asks God to promise that the temple will be a focal point of answered prayer for coming generations. Those prayers and God's promise also become a basis for the prayers of the generations that follow.

Finally, we will study one of the prayers of Daniel. Daniel too knew that God is to be approached on the basis of His promises. In the prayer we study, Daniel had discovered that God promised through the prophet Jeremiah that the exile in Babylon was to last for only a limited time: seventy years. So, Daniel prays, "How about it, God, you promised seventy years; it's been seventy years. Please do what you said."

Praying in the Promise

In these studies you will explore prayers that express humility and dignity. You will discover the needs of those who have great strengths. You will learn about longings that come from those who have reasons to be satisfied. Above all, you will see people who had the courage and strength to ask God to do what He promised.

As you read about these spiritual warriors who have gone before, I hope you will see how God has been working humility and dignity within you, how He has been exposing your needs and revealing your strengths, and that He has been working so that you can express longings in your soul that come from His satisfying presence. Above all, I hope that you will be able to ask God to do what He has promised. As you do, you will be learning the foundations for what it means to pray in Jesus' name.

1
Praying for Assurance

Genesis 15

Sensing a call to move our family to England, we had packed up our bags and our boys for a two-year mission assignment to work with American students studying in London. But as the two years neared an end, I couldn't see the next step. We were moving back to the States with no job to return to. Occasionally I struggled with panic. First I felt the weight of my family: how was I going to provide for them? Second, I felt the weight of a career change: I knew it was time to change from a campus minister to pastor of a church.

Questions tumbled through my mind: How long would it take to find a new position once we got back? Had I been irresponsible to take a call to another country when there was no clear next step after that time was over? Should I have written more letters and made more calls back to the U.S. in pursuit of a position?

Along with the questions were my prayers. Sometimes they took the form of questions: "God, where are You? We followed You over here, why aren't You leading us back?" Then there were fervent pleas for deliverance, guidance, comfort, and assurance. Every time I prayed, the issues surrounding our impending move displaced my previously disciplined prayers for friends, extended family, and Christian ministry.

One weekend the struggle inside me simply went away and the prayers for help and guidance seemed suddenly inappropriate.

Nothing outwardly had changed. No offer for a job came in the mail. I just *knew* that it was going to be all right. There was a quiet conviction inside that allowed me to trust God for what I couldn't yet see — and had not yet received. I knew that since I had trusted Him to lead us to one side of the Atlantic, I could trust Him to get us back.

In this passage of Scripture you will look at Abraham as he faced the problems of settling into a new land. In the process of settling in, he had a few questions for God. It is exciting to discover just how God responded.

1. Try to remember a time when you were waiting for something you really wanted — but hadn't yet received. What were some of your thoughts and feelings?

Read aloud Genesis 15

2. Focus on verse 1. Considering that Abram had already followed God to a strange new country, how might God's words be assuring?

3. Abram doesn't seem all that reassured by God's promises of verse 1. How would you describe his response to God in verses 2-6?

Look more carefully at verse 8. What else is Abram asking for?

4. Describe God's response to Abram's requests in verses 4-5 and 7.

5. How would you describe the relationship between God and Abram if the only information you had was verse 6?

In what ways is faith involved in our own relationship to God?

6. Although God gives Abram assurances, He doesn't immediately grant his requests. According to verses 14 and 16, what issues and obstacles was God going to have to deal with before giving Abram what he asked?

7. Consider some of your recent prayer requests. What issues and obstacles might God have to deal with in His response to your prayers?

8. In verses 12-16, what was both assuring and unsettling about God's promise that Abram's descendants would inherit the land?

9. Through the animals and the vision of a smoking firepot, God "cuts a covenant" with Abram in verses 17-19. This was a common way of making a binding contract. The responsible parties walked between the cut-up animals and in so doing implied that they too would be cut up if the commitments were not kept. What does it say about the character of God that He was the only One who went between the animals?

10. God gave Abram a covenant to provide a bond of personal commitment. What things has God given to all believers to assure us that He is committed to us?

11. Abram was motivated to pray because of his need for assurance. Consider your recent prayers; what have you asked for?

What responses have you gotten from God?

Abram needed assurance from God. What are some of the underlying motives of your prayers?

Scripture Memory

Abram believed the L*ord*, *and He credited it to him as righteousness.*
—Genesis 15:6

Prayer Project

Focus: Learning to trust God and to pray for the assurance of His constant care

✦ **Day One**
Read Genesis 15.
What problems are you facing for which you need God's help?

How do you think your life will be different if God answers your prayers?

Write out a prayer asking God to teach you how to pray for His continuing care during a time of waiting.

◆ **Day Two**
Read Genesis 15.
How has God answered your prayers in the past?

Can you recall any fervent requests that you have made which still go unanswered?

Write out your prayer asking God to give you assurance that He has heard your needs, fears, and desires.

◆ **Day Three**
Read Genesis 15.
God gave Abram a sense of assurance by taking him out to look at the stars. Spend some time outdoors in a natural setting. Ask God to give you a sense of encouragement by something about the world that He has made.

◆ **Day Four**
Read Genesis 15.
Before God gave Abram the assurance of the covenant, He had Abram collect and prepare the animals for sacrifice. Write out a prayer asking God what He might require of you as preparation to receive the encouragement you want.

◆ **Day Five**
Abram believed God. Write out your expression of faith. Tell God that you believe He has heard your requests and that you trust Him with your dreams, fears, and desires.

2
The Prayer
of Responsibility

Exodus 33:7-23

I wear several hats. Depending on the time of day and who I am
with, I am: a father, a husband, a pastor, a friend, a brother, or a
son. On some days, I change hats easily and without much
thought. But there are times when I become aware of the burdens
of responsibility.

Today I don't feel like I've done such a hot job of balancing my
roles as a pastor and a father. As my two older boys move into the
last stages of high school I feel at a loss to give them what a father
should. Part of the reason I struggle with this is that I am away
from them more than I should be.

On the other hand, I also have more to do at the church than I can
possibly do. I'm grateful that I am a member of a vital church and
that there are two other pastors and numbers of lay leaders with
whom I share ministry responsibilities. Still, there are tasks not
being covered that I should take on.

On days like today, when I am feeling the conflicting pull of com-
peting responsibilities, I have a choice. I can let these conflicts press
me down into a sense of despair, or I can let them take me down to
my knees in prayer. Today, I chose to pray. Calling out this morn-
ing with a sense of need, I was met with a sense of Presence.
Praying through the activities and agendas of the past week, I began
to see ways that God has been active and present. I felt my spirit lift
as I realized that God was meeting me, shaping me, and challenging

me to new growth. After my prayer time, I didn't feel any more competent than I had before I started, but I knew that my responsibilities weren't mine alone.

In the passage you are about to study, you will see Moses bearing the weight of responsibility for the leadership of Israel. As you read, you will get an intimate glimpse into his quiet time with God as he calls out for help. And God graciously responds.

1. What anxieties do you struggle with as you fulfill your responsibilities?

Read aloud Exodus 33:7-23

2. In these verses we get a special glimpse of Moses, the servant and friend of God. Look through the passage again and then describe his relationship to God in your own words.

3. Kenneth Swanson writes in his book *Uncommon Prayer*, "God doesn't have favorites, but He does have intimates." What do you think it is like to be intimate with God?

How would you describe some of your own hopes or frustrations regarding intimacy with God?

4. As part of his leadership Moses set up a tent of meeting outside the camp where he could meet with God (verses 7-11). What effects did that have on the people?

5. We probably won't set up physical tents to meet with God, but what *can* we do to set a regular meeting place with God?

What effects might come to others through our personal times with God?

6. Study verses 12 and 13. What requests does Moses make of God and how would these requests help him handle his responsibilities?

7. Now look over verses 14-16. Why do you think Moses was concerned about the presence of God?

8. Moses felt that it was the presence of God that made Israel distinct. How is it possible to recognize the presence of God in a church?

How can we recognize the presence of God in a person?

9. Read again verses 18-23. How would you describe the interaction between Moses and God?

10. God only partially answers Moses' requests. What is significant about what Moses can and can't know?

11. How would Moses' glimpse of God help him shoulder his leadership responsibilities?

12. What do you think God might be showing you about Himself and what needs in your life might He be meeting as He does so?

Scripture Memory

The LORD replied "My Presence will go with you and I will give you rest."

—Exodus 33:14

Prayer Project

Focus: Learning to carry our responsibilities

✦ Day One
Read Exodus 33:7-23.
The tent of meeting was set up for Israelites to inquire of the Lord.
Let the focus of your prayers today be on asking God questions.
Write out as many questions as you can think of that you would
like God to answer.

✦ Day Two
Read Exodus 33:7-23.
Moses' prayer time was a meeting with God. As you come to God
today in prayer, be careful not to focus on gathering information or
telling God what you need. Plan to meet with God Person-to-
person. Silence is a helpful discipline to sharpen our spiritual senses.
Sit quietly for an extended period of time cultivating a listening,
responsive heart. After a while write down your impressions and
responses to your time of quiet.

✦ Day Three
Read Exodus 33:7-23.
One of the ways that God meets us and equips us for life is through our daily experiences. Think about your life for the past month or so. Write down as many experiences as you can think of, using just a word or two for each. (Don't worry about putting them in chronological order.) After you have written down all that comes to mind, ask God to show you His hand behind and through these experiences. As you reflect on these, write down any ideas, concerns, or thoughts that come to mind.

✦ Day Four
Read Exodus 33:7-23.
Pain and struggle are also means by which God makes His presence known to us. C.S. Lewis wrote that pain is God's megaphone. Think back over the past month or so. Write down any pains, struggles, or concerns that come to mind. How have these made you aware of God's presence in your life? How do you think God might be using these to empower you for your responsibilities?

✦ **Day Five**
Read Exodus 33:7-23.
Moses was equipped to lead the people because God promised His
continued presence and gave him a fresh revelation of His character.
Write out a prayer asking God to make Himself known to you in
fresh ways.

Consider ways that God has shown you about Himself recently.
Write what comes to mind and then spend several minutes in
thanksgiving and worship.

3
Persistent Prayer

Psalm 34

There is something about prayer that seems to put us off. Ever notice how we edge around it? When you attend a prayer meeting, note the ratio of time spent talking about prayer with the amount of time spent in prayer. If there are fifteen minutes set aside for prayer, you will talk about what to pray for twelve minutes with only three left over to pray. If sixty minutes are set aside for prayer, generally the first fifty minutes will be consumed with discussion and perhaps the last ten minutes will be spent praying.

What is going on here? Why the edgy avoidance? Why do we want to talk around prayer rather than do it? I'm not sure, but I know that even when I look at the prayer patterns of my own life I find the same tendency. Sometimes I notice it in the time I set aside to pray. I am always letting other scheduled demands crowd it out. Sometimes I notice it, not in the amount of time I spend in prayer, but in the way I pray. Instead of lifting my heart to God, reaching in and up in the pursuit of His help, I allow my prayers to become routine times of repeated phrases and current spiritual clichés — outward forms with little spiritual substance.

Great spiritual teachers are those who have the ability to inspire us to pray again. They help us to see that we have somehow (we hardly notice when it happens) fallen out of prayer as a way of life. More than that, great spiritual teachers elicit from us a hunger to pray again. David is such a teacher. In Psalm 34 he writes to inspire us to prayer. Through sharing his own experiences of answered prayer he entices us to the heartfelt, soul-driven experience of prayer to the Living God.

1. How do you feel when someone invites you to join in the fun at a party?

Read aloud Psalm 34:1-3

2. David invites us to enter into his celebration of God. What words does David use to describe his enthusiasm for God?

How do those words affect you?

3. The cause of David's celebration is answered prayer, "I sought the LORD and He answered me." Look at verses 4, 6-7, 17, and 19. What do you think David wanted from the Lord?

4. Looking over the phrases for prayer in the whole Psalm, how would you describe the emotional tone of David's prayers: quiet? confident? passive? intense? insistent? fearful? (Feel free to add adjectives of your own.) Choose several adjectives, then explain why you chose them.

5. How does the tone of your prayers compare with David's?

What can you learn about prayer from David's example?

6. Study verses 8-10. David's answered prayer causes him to re-flect on the benefits of a life with God, "Taste and see that the LORD is good." What might prayer have to do with opening up our ability to spiritually taste and see?

7. According to verse 10, David is confident that those who "seek the LORD" won't lack anything good. How may seeking the Lord be different from merely asking God to meet your needs and grant your requests?

8. Focus on verses 11-14. There is a relationship between our moral character and God's answers to our prayers. What re-quirements are mentioned here?

Illustrate how such behavior might look in everyday life by giving several examples.

9. Read again verses 15-22. What assurances for answered prayer does David offer?

Why do you think he felt it necessary to offer such assurances?

10. How does David help us to see that the pursuit of prayer often comes from a life of need and pain?

11. How have your struggles affected the way that you pray?

12. Considering Psalm 34, how would you describe the relationship between faith and persevering prayer?

What are you currently pursuing God for?

Scripture Memory

I sought the LORD, *and He answered me; He delivered me from all my fears.*

—Psalm 34:4

Prayer Project

Focus: Praying persistent, heartfelt prayer

Answered prayer comes from the pursuit of God. Each day this week be prepared to intentionally reach out to God.

✦ Day One
What needs or threats are you currently facing? Write them down and note how they make you feel.

Needs   *Threats*   *Challenges*   *Emotions*

✦ Day Two
Write a brief note to God telling Him of your needs and why you want Him to answer you. Include in your letter why you think He should answer you and how you think your life will be affected if He doesn't.

Date:

Dear God,

Fervently,

✦ Day Three

In Luke 11 Jesus instructed His disciples in prayer by telling a parable about a person who kept knocking on a friend's door at midnight to get bread for some unexpected guests. Read Luke 11:1-10. Place yourself in the role of the one who is knocking.

How do you feel to have to keep on knocking?

What fears or hesitations do you have?

Why do you keep on doing it?

What might happen if you stop?

✦ Day Four

In Luke 18:1-8 Jesus tells the parable of the persistent widow. The woman pesters an unjust judge until he finally grants her justice. Read it and place yourself in the role of the widow.

How do you feel about having to pursue God to answer your prayers?

How is it affecting your relationship to Him?

How is it affecting the way you approach your problems?

How is it affecting the way you view yourself: your abilities, character, motivations?

✦ Day Five

One of the mysteries and frustrations about prayer is that some of our prayers get answered and some seem to go unanswered. We can find courage to keep praying by recalling prayers God has answered.

What prayers has God answered for you?

What difference did it make in your life?

Write out several expressions of gratitude.

Tell God that you are anxious to be delivered from your frustrations but are willing to trust Him until He does.

4
A Prayer
of Consecration

1 Chronicles 29:1-20

Prayer is not only communication with God, it is also a consecration to God. When we consecrate something we set it aside from normal use and reserve it for a special relationship with God. The act of prayer is setting aside time that we would use for other purposes and devoting it to time alone with our Creator. This is the first act of consecration and without it our spiritual growth will remain insignificantly small.

Prayer, however, is not only an act of consecration, but the means by which we consecrate. By means of prayer we can set aside our family, our house, our work, anything, to be devoted to God's purposes rather than our own. When we pray in this way we enter into a partnership and service of God that calls us beyond ourselves to the tasks of eternity. Our spiritual growth is stretched to its limits.

One of the most important (and difficult) prayers of consecration is the consecration of our money. David was forbidden by God to build the temple because of his life as a warrior—he was a man of blood. But David determined that if he couldn't build the temple, his son Solomon would have all the resources and plans for the temple sitting on the shelf and ready to go when the time came. At the end of his life, David worked and prayed toward that end.

I am challenged by David's example. Our church is in the middle of a fund-raising drive to buy the property next door. It's a great opportunity for us to grow; we could certainly use the space. But it means that we've got to come up with the funds, and that can be no fun! From the fancy financial footwork of Ananias and Sapphira in the early days of the church, to the faulty fund-raising of indulgences in the 16th Century, to the financial scandals of today, the church has had its problems with money and building campaigns. When church leaders ask for money, eyebrows go up and arms fold across the chest. I tell the suspicious that there is good reason to be cautious—but not closed. David shows us that the freedom to give money is both the expression of a consecrated heart and the means by which our hearts can become consecrated.

In the passage you study here you will see how money and prayer are brought together in the service of God. Prayers of consecration open new areas of your life to give over to God's use and blessing.

1. How do you respond to solicitation for funds for a church program or Christian ministry?

Read aloud 1 Chronicles 29:1-5
2. David is setting in motion a massive building campaign that will continue far beyond his death. How does he go about getting his people to participate?

Read aloud verses 6-9
3. People generally are not eager to give away their financial resources. What could account for the overwhelming response to David's appeal for funds?

Read aloud verses 10-13

4. David responds to the people's generosity with a prayer of consecration. Note the words he uses to praise God and then rephrase his praise in your own words.

5. The stimulus for David's prayer was the generous response of Israel's leaders. From these verses, how might the generosity of people and the generosity of God be interconnected?

How might contributing to a ministry or mission help us keep not only our possessions, but our entire relationship to God, in proper perspective?

Read aloud the rest of David's prayer in verses 14-19

6. What clues do you see here about the role prayer might play in the process of making an offering to God?

7. Focus on verses 14-16. How does David's prayer reflect a healthy balance of humility and pride?

In what ways can our prayers be a form of unhealthy humility and false pride?

8. Read verse 17. David rejoices that the gifts were given willingly and with an honest intent. What other motives are there for making a contribution to the Lord's ministry?

9. In verses 18-19, David prays for Israel and for his son, Solomon. What parallels might there be between the future condition of the temple and the future condition of their hearts?

10. David knows that the human heart has a tendency to grow spiritually cool. Has this ever happened to you?

How did you respond?

How might prayer and giving be a means of addressing a cool heart?

11. Consecration is the act of setting aside something to be devoted to God (money, time, skills, objects like a car or a house). What acts of consecration might God be calling you to?

The consecration of the people empowered the building of the temple. What do you think your consecration might empower? .

Scripture Memory

Wealth and honor come from You; You are the ruler of all things. In Your hands are strength and power to exalt and give strength to all.
— 1 Chronicles 29:12

Prayer Project

Focus: Prayers of Consecration

You may find the prayer exercises this week especially challenging. Each day you will be encouraged to consecrate new aspects of your life to God. Allow yourself time to prayerfully think through each area. Be careful. Don't make commitments to God that you don't feel ready to.

Each day be sure that you allow adequate time to become quiet and inwardly settled. You may find that your prayers and reflections will bring up thoughts and feelings that were deep inside you. Make notes about your responses in the space provided and be prepared to write further reflections in a journal. You might even find you would benefit by sharing your responses with a trusted friend.

✦ Day One
Consecrating Yourself
Consider your past: There may be some things about it that you feel good about but others that you regret and even resent. Acknowledge that God was present with you and can use your past for His purposes and for your good.

• In the space provided, jot down memories that come to you.

When you are ready say, "Lord, I give my past to you."

- Consider your future: What dreams and hopes do you have? Write them down.

When you are ready say, "Lord, I give my future to you."

- One by one, spend time consecrating each of the following areas:

Consecrate your body.

Consecrate your mind.

Consecrate your talents and gifts.

✦ Day Two
Consecrating Your Family
We didn't choose our families of origin; they were chosen for us. This may be a source of pleasure, pain, or a mixture of both. Regardless of how you feel, by giving your family over to God you honor Him and allow Him to work His blessings.

- One by one think and pray through each relationship, consecrating each to the Lord when you are ready.

Your mother

Your father

Your siblings

Significant extended family members

• If you are married think and pray through the following relationships. If you aren't married but hope to be, you can still consecrate to God these future potential relationships.

Your spouse

Your children

◆ **Day Three**
Consecrating Your Possessions
Seek today to give over every physical thing you own to God. Keep
in mind that you are telling God that everything you have belongs
to Him and is at His disposal. You are expressing a willingness to
give away money for ministries or to meet needs of others — if you
sense that is what God is calling you to do.

• Consider your regular income. Write down how much you get.

Consider how you use it.

Tell God you are consecrating it to Him.

Ask Him if there are different ways that He wants you to use it.
Consider if there is a portion of your income that He wants you
to use in a specific way.

- Consider your savings and investments. Write down how much you have.

Thank God for what He has allowed you to accumulate. Tell Him you are giving Him the freedom to use it as He sees fit. Ask Him if there is any portion of it He wants to use for ministry or service projects.

- Consider your house, car, and clothes. Take a guess at how much financial worth you have in them.

Thank God for His blessings in this area. Acknowledge that all you have comes from Him. Dedicate them to His use.

✦ Day Four
Consecrating Your Work
Consider your job. Thank God for the work He allows you to do and the abilities that you use. Reflect on all that is involved in your work and give over each area to the Lord.

- Your supervisors

- Your peers

- Your projects and tasks

- Your successes

- Your failures and setbacks

✦ **Day Five**

Consecrating Your Leisure

God thinks our leisure time is important; that's why He created the Sabbath. Before our leisure can truly become a time of re-creation and refreshment, however, it too needs to be consecrated.

• Think through how you use your "free" time. Thank God for it and ask Him to show you how He would like you to use it.

• Consecrate your regular days off from work.

• Consecrate your vacation time. Ask God to make them true holy-days.

• Consecrate your relaxation and fun activities. Ask God to use the times of fun and relaxation to be a means of exploring His grace and goodness.

5

The Promise and Place of Prayer

1 Kings 8:22-40

While I am immersed in a project, one of my sons intrudes into my concentration with a request that I take him to a movie. I enjoy spending time with him, but I prefer to do it on my own terms. More than likely my response will be something like "Not now, I want to finish this first." Of course the problem with that response is that my project may take longer than I intended. More often than I like to admit, my son's requests may get put off—and then forgotten.

The one thing that arrests me in the midst of my project is the phrase "You promised." At that point, if I in fact did promise, I must put down my screwdriver or turn off my computer. I have made a prior commitment that I need to fulfill. I follow my son out the door.

One of the amazing gifts of God to His people is His willingness to make a promise. (The Old Testament uses the word *covenant* to express this concept.) In a covenant, God is willing to be held accountable.

As you will see in this study of Solomon's dedicatory prayer of the temple, calling on God's promise is the foundation of prayer. God is not offended that we ask Him to do what He has promised to do. In fact, when we appeal to God's promises in prayer we honor God's trustworthy character and increase our own assurance that we will be heard and helped.

1. How do you feel when someone asks you to fulfill a promise that you have made?

Read aloud 1 Kings 8:22-40

2. Focus on verses 22-26. Biblical prayer is rooted in the character and promises of God. What promises from God does Solomon mention here?

3. Why is appealing to the promises of God one good way to begin prayer?

   How might the character of God, as it is described in these verses, encourage prayer?

4. Look more closely at verses 27-30. In what ways does Solomon link prayer and the temple?

   Why might Solomon think that having a special place of prayer will be helpful?

5. What aids have you found helpful in your times of prayer?

6. Solomon sees prayer as a means of coping with problems. Skim verses 31-40 and identify the future problems that he hopes prayer will be a means of addressing.

7. What problems do you tend to take to God in prayer?

Are there areas of your life or problems that you don't seem to pray about? Why not?

8. Solomon addresses four central problems in verses 31-40. What are the causes of those problems and how is prayer a means to remedy them?

9. What role does sin and forgiveness play in the vitality of your prayer life?

10. In verse 38, Solomon mentions "the spreading out of hands" as a posture of prayer. Note verse 22 where he uses the same posture as he begins his own prayer. How might the spreading out of hands be a helpful position in which to pray?

    What is your own favored posture of prayer and why do you prefer it?

11. Spend some time now in prayer. As you pray consider your prayer posture, the promises of God, your problems, and God's grace.

Scripture Memory

O LORD, *God of Israel, there is no God like You in heaven above or on earth below — You who keep Your covenant of love with Your servants who continue wholeheartedly in Your way.*

—1 Kings 8:23

Prayer Project

Focus: Learning to pray by appealing to the promises of God.

✦ Day One
The Promise of His Presence
The most fundamental human need is to know that we are not alone. Throughout history God's people have found that it is the divine Presence that binds up our deepest wounds and gives strength and courage to face our greatest challenges.

Read Joshua 1:1-5 and write out what it says.

Read Matthew 28:16-20 and write out what it says.

Consider times when you have felt alone in the past; when was it and how did you feel?

What difference would it make in the way you feel and act if you know in your head and your heart that God is with you right now?

Claim the promises that Jesus offers in Matthew 28:16-20. Write out your prayer.

✦ Day Two
The Promise of His Mission

Every human has a need for a sense of purpose, a cause bigger than our own personal needs. The good news is that every Christian has such a purpose: serving God and bearing witness to Christ's kingdom. The day-to-day issues of life, however, can take our attention away from that broader purpose. Life can collapse into a series of dull details and pressing tasks that urgently demand our attention but sap energy and enthusiasm.

Reread Joshua 1:1-5. Write these verses in your own words, paying special attention to the purpose God had for Joshua.

Reread Matthew 28:16-20. Write out these verses in your own words, paying special attention to the purpose that God had for the disciples.

Write a prayer of your own claiming God's promise of a special purpose for your life.

✦ Day Three
The Promise of His Provision

For many of us, earning a living is not easy. Whether it is hunting for game, growing crops, or going to the office, there are traps, weeds, and stresses that we must face. God never intended, however, that we do this on our own. Even as we work we are to ask and then be open to receive with gratitude what He provides.

Read Luke 11:3. Write out what you understand this verse to mean.

Read Luke 12:13-21. Summarize the main points.

Read Luke 12:22-34. Summarize the main points.

Based on what you have read, write out a prayer requesting that God meet your personal needs.

✦ Day Four

The Promise of His Forgiveness

We live in a moral universe. In spite of the efforts of our modern culture to make truth and morality relative, we still have an inbuilt sense of right and wrong. The result is a compelling inner sense of "shoulds" and "oughts" that never leave us alone. In a word, we all have to cope with a sense of guilt. Some try to rationalize it away and reduce it to mere feelings. Others try to cover over it with a torrent of activities in work and play. The best way to deal with it is the Christian way: to come to God and admit we are guilty and then accept the gift of grace that comes through the Cross.

Read Mark 2:1-12. What can you discover here about the dynamics of sickness, guilt, grace, faith, and health?

Read 1 John 1:8-10. Summarize what it says.

Make a list of all the things for which you feel guilty. After you have done it, write a prayer claiming the promise of forgiveness.

✦ Day Five
The Promise of His Wisdom

No matter how bright or experienced we are, there is always more to life than we can figure out. We need the wisdom of God if we are to make good decisions. God promises that wisdom to those who seek Him.

Read James 1:5-8. What is required to receive the wisdom of God?

Read Proverbs 3:5-8. What is required to receive God's wisdom?

Write out a prayer telling God what you are going to do to meet His conditions for wisdom. After you have told God what you are going to do, tell God in what areas you need wisdom and ask that it be given to you.

6
The Prayer of Prevailing Pursuit

Daniel 9:1-19

Before my conversion I used to think that people who had to pray for divine aid were weak-willed and incompetent. Just before and after my conversion I encountered people who demonstrated just how wrong I was.

On the night the Lord got through to me I listened to the testimony of several competent businessmen. They told stories of how God had rescued them from financial disaster. They were certain that prayer was the only means to account for the last-minute turnaround in their fortunes. That got me thinking that perhaps it was OK to pray after all. With that slightly open door God stepped through and met me in a way I had thought never could happen.

Six weeks after my conversion I went to Haiti with a mission team from my new church. We lived with another group of missionaries for a couple of weeks. I was shocked to discover how capable they were. My stereotypes crumbled. I began to understand that people who prayed didn't do so because they didn't know what they were doing. Rather, they prayed because they *did* know what they were doing. They didn't pray because they were humanly weak-willed and incompetent, but because they were strong enough to seek God.

In the prayer of Daniel that you are about to study, you will meet a highly competent official of the government of Babylon. He was so highly valued that, despite the prejudice against the Jewish race and religion, this Jew was an intimate advisor to the king. Daniel could do a lot of things well, but what he did best was pray. He prayed when it was against the law to pray. He prayed when he faced death by lions. He prayed when confronted by strange dreams. And he prayed when he discovered a promise about the restoration of Jerusalem buried in a scroll of the prophet Jeremiah. You will be studying his prayer for the restoration. Pay attention because you will see how a man of power approaches the God of all power. His prayer for his nation set events in motion that ultimately brought about a second Exodus of Judah from a foreign land.

1. Recall a time when you had to admit that you had done something wrong. How did you feel?

What happened when you tried to set things straight?

Read aloud Daniel 9:1-19

2. Describe the tone of Daniel's prayer.

3. According to verses 1-2, what motivated Daniel to pray?

4. Notice in verse 3 the conditions of Daniel's prayer. How might fasting, sackcloth, and ashes have been helpful aids to Daniel's praying?

5. We don't generally use such aids to prayer as fasting or sackcloth. Why not?

What ways are available for us to outwardly express our prayers?

6. Look more carefully at verses 4-6. Daniel begins his prayer for mercy by acknowledging guilt. In what specific ways has Israel failed to keep the covenant with God?

7. Study verses 7-11. What phrases here show the extent of Israel's guilt?

8. Daniel identifies with Judah's sins of the past. Although Daniel himself was a godly man, in verse 7 he says, "We are covered with shame." What can you learn from his example?

How will Daniel benefit if God answers his prayers?

What personal benefits will come to you if your intercessory prayers for others are answered?

9. Review verses 11-14. How do Israel's troubles demonstrate that God has been faithful to the covenant?

10. How might the experience of God's judgment bring us a deeper sense of security and trust?

How can the knowledge of God's judgment enhance our prayer life?

11. Read again verses 15-19. To what does Daniel appeal as he asks God to restore the city of Jerusalem?

12. Throughout Daniel's prayer there is a sense that God can be persuaded to act in spite of Judah's sin. What do you see of boldness and also of humility in his approach to God?

13. Spend some time in prayer now. Try to approach God with the same sense of boldness and humility that you saw in Daniel. Pray for people and problems that need God's help.

Scripture Memory

O Lord, the great and awesome God, who keeps His covenant of love with all who love Him and obey His commands, we have sinned and done wrong. . . . we have turned away from your commands and laws.
— Daniel 9:4-5

Prayer Project

Focus: To practice praying for others

Each day you will pray for a different group of people. The chart for each day requires you to do some reflection on whom you are praying for. If you need more space, try enlarging each chart in your journal. You will need to consider what scriptural promise you can appeal to, what areas of sin you can identify with and confess, what needs each person has, and what outcomes you would like to see happen.

If you take time to work through the chart for each group you will find that praying for others requires forethought and spiritual effort. You might find yourself drained when you are through. That's OK. For some people or issues, you might find you are weighed down and burdened. That's normal too. You will be discovering that praying for others is much more than merely mentioning their names as you move through a shopping list of people and their needs.

◆ Day One
Pray for your family

Names/Issues	God's promise to which you appeal	Disobedience to God that needs His forgiveness	Needs and problems you want God to address	Outcomes you would like to see

✦ Day Two
Pray for your church

Names/Issues	God's promise to which you appeal	Disobedience to God that needs His forgiveness	Needs and problems you want God to address	Outcomes you would like to see

✦ Day Three
Pray for your work

Names/Issues	God's promise to which you appeal	Disobedience to God that needs His forgiveness	Needs and problems you want God to address	Outcomes you would like to see

✦ Day Four
Pray for your neighborhood

Names/Issues	God's promise to which you appeal	Disobedience to God that needs His forgiveness	Needs and problems you want God to address	Outcomes you would like to see

✦ Day Five
Pray for our world

Names/Issues	God's promise to which you appeal	Disobedience to God that needs His forgiveness	Needs and problems you want God to address	Outcomes you would like to see

Notes for Leaders

Preparation

Begin your preparation with prayer and personal study. Prepare to lead your particular lesson by following the ten steps under *Suggestions for Personal Study* beginning on page 8.

Study the biblical context of the passage under consideration. Research any questions likely to sidetrack your group.

Study the flow of questions. TruthSeed questions are designed to create a flow of discussion from beginning to end. Get comfortable with the potential directions of the study. Mark pacing notes so that the discussion will spread evenly over your allotted time. Most TruthSeed studies should last about an hour.

Read the leader's notes for your particular study beginning on page 66. Mark information that you may need during the course of the study in the blank spaces of your question list.

If your group time includes other ingredients such as refreshments, music, worship, sharing, and prayer, plan time divisions so that your group is able to accomplish all that is scheduled. Many TruthSeed lessons make suggestions for these additional ingredients at the close of the Bible study section.

Acknowledge to yourself and to God that the group belongs to the people in it, not to you as a leader. TruthSeed is designed to facilitate a group discovery form of learning moderated by a discussion leader. Plan to lead with the group's welfare and interests in mind.

Pray for each group member by name.

Group Time

Begin on time. No apology necessary. The group has come together for a particular purpose and has assigned you the job of leading it in the study.

If your group is meeting for the first time, survey together the suggestions for group discussion on page 7. This will help each person to know what is expected and will get you off on a common footing.

Take appropriate note of the narrative introduction at the beginning of the study, then ask the opening question. Encourage responses from each person. When everyone seems involved in the subject at hand, the group will be ready to enter the biblical text. Since the opening questions point toward the text but do not interact with it, always ask the opening question BEFORE reading the Scripture.

Read the assigned Scripture passage aloud. Or ask several group members to read. Some people feel embarrassed about their reading skills, so don't make surprise assignments unless you are certain that they will be well accepted. Paragraph breaks in the text mark natural thought divisions, so always read by paragraphs, not by verses.

Conduct a discussion of the biblical text using the questions supplied. TruthSeed questions should promote multiple answers and group interaction. Allow time for several people to respond to each question and to each other. If the group does not seem to understand a particular question, rephrase it until it becomes clear, break it into smaller units, or give a brief summary and move on.

Give encouraging comments. If an answer is partially right, acknowledge that part. If an answer seems inappropriate, say something like, "What verse led you to that conclusion?" or "What do some of the rest of you think?"

Don't be afraid of silence. Help group members to become comfortable with the quiet by announcing a "thinking time." Then invite them to share their thoughtful responses to the questions at hand. Learn a sensitivity to God that can come from occasional silence.

Pace the study. It is the leader's responsibility to be sure that you finish on time and that the group has adequate time to discuss later questions. Some questions will take longer than others, so create a flexible pace with one eye on the clock and the other on interests of your group. Don't be afraid to redirect attention to the question list or the biblical text. Suggest that you may come back to some interesting topic after you have finished the study.

Involve everyone—more or less equally. Draw in quiet people by asking for nonthreatening opinion responses. Avoid direct eye contact with someone who talks a bit too much. If necessary, point out the shared responsibility for a successful discussion by reading item 4 on page 7.

Avoid over-talking yourself. Groups with an overactive leader get tempted to sit back and let the leader do *all* the work. Eventually, this causes people to lose the benefit of a personal encounter with the Scripture as it impacts their own lives.

Keep the discussion on track. Consider writing the purpose statement from the leader's section at the top of your question page so that you can keep the discussion objective in mind. You can head off a tangent by gently directing attention back to the biblical text. But do consider the relative merit of any potential tangent. Sometimes apparent tangents represent real needs that the group ought to address. In that case, adjust your plan (for the moment) and follow the needs of the group. If the tangent seems of limited interest or importance, offer to talk about it in more detail at a later time. Or if the tangent is of great importance, but requires further preparation, ask the group to table it for this session, but come back to it at a later meeting.

Don't skip questions of personal application. Here is where Scripture does its most important work. As other group members respond, be ready to add your own experiences of God's work in your life.

Open and close your study with prayer. Or ask someone in your group to do so.

Study One

Praying for Assurance

Genesis 15

Purpose: To discover how God responds to our prayers and provides assurance for us even as He requires us to wait for His answers.

Background. Abram probably didn't know a great deal about God before God called him from his home in Ur of Chaldees. It was over the course of years of experience with God that he came to know and trust Him. The account of Abram's life over Genesis 12–25 records his journey of faith and the changes that he went through.

In Genesis 15 Abram is still in the early stages of getting to know God. Although God has made promises to him, these promises have not yet come true. Then God comes to him with amazing expressions of reassurance.

Question 1. Help people in your group think about how anxiety affects them. You might also help them explore how prayers not yet answered affect them while they wait for answers.

Question 2. To help people think about this question ask what they felt like when they moved to a new location.

Question 3. Abram's two fundamental concerns were having children and a place for them to live. In that culture (in contrast to ours) having a child was supremely important—desired even above material possessions. It is also important to note that the land was densely populated with many different people groups. (See verse 19.)

Question 4. It is important to note that God is not necessarily put off or offended when we ask Him for assurance in a difficult situation. This chapter illustrates just how seriously God takes the cares and concerns of His people.

Question 5. This is one of the most significant verses in the Bible.

In Romans 4, the Apostle Paul uses this to show that righteousness from God has always been a gift given in response to faith.

Reflecting on this verse will help us see that although Abram asked for reassurance, his requests didn't come from a negative skepticism. Instead they were healthy expressions of faith-filled anxieties.

Question 7. Encourage members of your group to consider how their experiences may be divinely guided answers. This means that answering our requests may take years of shaping our immediate and future circumstances.

Question 9. Like verse 6, this is one of the most significant passages in the Bible. God makes His first covenant with Abram. In so doing, He shows that He is willing to make commitments that put His character on the line. Some theologians see God's willingness to enter covenants as so significant that they have built a system of theology upon it, called (appropriately enough) "Covenant Theology."

Question 10. God has given promises throughout the Scriptures that He hears our prayers. Supremely, the cross of Jesus Christ is the sign of assurance that God wants to meet our needs.

Question 11. You may find it helpful to ask for more than one response to the question on motives for prayer. It would also be helpful to encourage members to pause long enough to reflect on their inner desires. Asking people to jot down a couple of reasons may be a good way for them to recognize their motivations.

Study Two
The Prayer of Responsibility
Exodus 33:7-23

Purpose: To see how God responds to our prayers for help with the responsibilities of life.

Background. This passage follows the golden calf incident of Exodus 32. In response to Israel's idolatry, God punished them and threatened to withdraw His presence. Moses was caught in a diffi-cult situation, pulled between his devotion to God and the sense of responsibility that he felt toward the people he was to lead. It is easy to imagine that Moses was feeling alone and uncertain. In these verses we get insight into his intimate relationship with God as Moses vents his frustrations to God.

Question 1. This question allows people in your group to speak openly to each other. Used well, it can lead them to receive help from this passage of Scripture, but also to be more vulnerable and supportive with each other.

Question 2. The wonderful thing about the God of Christianity is that He is a personal God. The good news is not just that we can know Him but that He knows us. We see this in the Gospels as Jesus calls each disciple personally. It carries on in the Epistles as the Apostle Paul writes that believers are chosen in Christ before the creation of the world (See Ephesians 1:4.)

Question 3. It might be helpful to think about other people in Scripture who were God's intimates. I think of Abraham, Samuel, David, Peter, and Paul.

Question 5. This is an excellent opportunity to talk about the discipline of a regular quiet time. If people express a need for help, you might refer them to the *Spiritual Encounter Series* written to help people who want to grow in their quiet times. Direct them to the listing in *For Further Reading* on page 79.

Question 6. The knowledge of God is the most important thing we can pray for. Knowing that God is good would be a sure founda-tion for calling Israel to trust God. Jonathan Edwards wrote that goodness is the most important attribute of God. What would hap-pen if God were all powerful and omnipresent, but not good? How terrible and dangerous this god would be!

Question 7. In the Christian college I attended for part of my college career, people were concerned with dress codes as a means of keeping a good testimony. We were supposed to dress differently to show that we were different from the world. In that light I found these verses striking. That which distinguishes God's people from the world is not some outward way of dressing but the presence of God Himself among them.

Question 8. This is the dilemma of serving God. Although we can't see Him, He is present. Although He is beyond our physical senses, we can still know that He is present. Some people in your group may have had the experience of being in a dead church where all the right actions were present and even the right doctrines, yet there was little sense of living faith and heart-warming worship. Encourage group members to speak of evidences they have seen of God's presence in a church or in people.

Question 9. This is one of Scripture's most graphic pictures of God's interaction with a human. Encourage your group to give factual descriptions from the text as well as emotional responses to the scene it presents.

Question 10. The note for question 8 may help give perspective to this question.

Question 11. This question sets up the follow-up exercise to be used through the week.

Study Three
Persistent Prayer
Psalm 34

Purpose: To help us overcome resistance to persistent, heartfelt prayers.

Question 1. This question will help your group enter into David's experience of answered prayer. Sometimes it's hard to enter into a celebration of another's blessings. We may stand back and be passive observers saying, "That's nice for you, but how does that affect me?" The nature of spiritual blessings, however, is that they are contagious. If we open up to another's joy, it becomes ours as well. Help members of the group think of times when they may have experienced this sort of contagious spiritual experience.

Question 2. This is a simple question, but important. It helps us feel David's enthusiasm for seeking God in prayer. After the members have mentioned the words *extol, praise, boast, rejoice, glorify, exalt,* help them think about what each means.

Question 4. It is not unusual for people to think of prayer merely as requests to God, void of any sort of relational or emotional content. Nothing could be further from the truth. This question may help people see how emotion-laden David's prayers were.

Question 5. Help people explore the emotional and relational dynamics of their own prayers.

Question 6. David invites us to spiritual sensations, to "taste and see." The invitation sounds strange to our physically satiated, consumer-oriented culture. Because of this, it's a difficult question. It could, however, open the door to thinking and feeling something new and deeper in the experience of knowing the goodness of God.

Question 7. Seeking God requires a sense of intention and pursuit. Jesus conveys the same idea in the parable of the persistent widow recorded in Luke 18:1-8, or the parable of the friend in need in Luke 11:5-10. God is most pleased with prayers that come from a hungry, determined heart. Passive prayers offered with little sense of need or desire fall short of seeking God.

Question 8. One of the reasons we avoid prayer is that we know we fall short of the righteousness that God requires. That is why, as Christians, we pray in the name of Jesus whose death on the cross atones for our moral failures. Encourage people to consider reasons why they may avoid prayer.

Question 10. Your group should draw answers from throughout the Psalm. Victories in prayer arise out of life's battles. The promise of answered prayer is not that it keeps us from trouble or pain, but that God aids us in our struggles.

Question 12. Our faith continually grows and deepens throughout our Christian pilgrimage to heaven. This does not guarantee that the mature saint gets prayers answered more rapidly than does a young believer. It should mean that the mature saint can endure longer waits and greater struggles as God carries out His will in us and through us.

Study Four
A Prayer of Consecration
1 Chronicles 29:1-20

Purpose: To consider ways that prayer can help us bring more of our life under the lordship of Christ so that we can be open to acts of obedience and service with all of our resources.

Question 1. Aim for both positive and negative responses, but try to keep members from evaluating each other. Allow each person the freedom to have his or her own opinion without requiring others to agree.

Question 2. David sets the tone as a good leader should. He demonstrates that he is not only willing to allocate the resources of the crown to the project, but personal funds as well. David remained, throughout his life, an eager, devoted worshiper of God.

Question 3. Someone in your group may express concern about the vast amount of wealth described here. Numbers written in Hebrew are frequently difficult to translate. Even if we don't know the exact amount, we can get the point—David gave generously.

Question 4. David was a skillful worshiper and had all kinds of words of celebration and praise in his vocabulary. Paying attention to David's words will challenge us to develop a vocabulary of praise as well.

Question 5. Encourage members to consider how they feel when they have made a contribution to a church or Christian ministry.

Question 6. As he prays David acknowledges God as the source of all things and the eternal Creator of life. Implicitly, all prayer acknowledges that God has power and resources that we don't.

Question 7. While it is an expression of humility to acknowledge that all comes from God, there is also an implicit sense of dignity that comes when we understand that God chooses to share His resources with us. Being important to God makes us important.

Question 8. Among other things, giving may be a source of control or public status. This may be a threatening question; probe but don't push. What other ways can your group think of?

Question 9. History demonstrated that Solomon did not live all his life with a devoted heart. After his death his kingdom was divided, his family continued in his divided ways. Eventually the temple fell into disrepair and was destroyed by the Babylonians.

Question 10. Try to set a tone that allows people to talk about their "cool" periods—without being judged.

Question 11. The depth of conversation triggered by this question will depend on how safe members of your group feel with each other. Encourage members to take some risk by trying to draw them out. Be sensitive, however, to what trust level the group can handle.

Study Five
The Promise and Place of Prayer
1 Kings 8:22-40

Purpose: To grow in the power of prayer by learning to appeal to the promises of God.

Question 2. Solomon is referring to several covenants in this passage. Verse 23 speaks of the covenant of love expressed in the Ten Commandments: "But showing love to a thousand generations of those who love me and keep my commandments" (Exodus 20:6). Verse 24 refers to God's promise to David to let Solomon build the temple. Verse 25 recalls God's promise to keep one of David's descendants on the throne of Israel. (See 1 Chronicles 28:4-7.)

We find assurance for our prayers because God makes and keeps His promises as is demonstrated by the fact that Solomon, the son of David, was on the throne as he prayed this prayer. In contrast, God made no such promise to Saul and, as a result, the sons of Saul were displaced by David. (See 2 Samuel 5:1-4.)

Question 3. Jesus said that spiritual power is unleashed according to our faith. (See Mark 5:34, 36; 9:23.) Knowing that God makes and keeps His promises is an aid to strengthen our faith. Appealing to God's promises also focuses our prayers. We are to pray in accordance with God's will—not merely for whatever whim and wish that we might have. Your group should come to these or similar conclusions.

Question 4. Solomon hopes that God will make the temple a visible focus of prayer. He asks not merely that prayers prayed within the temple would be heard by God, but that prayers prayed *toward* the temple would be heard as well. This is Solomon's way of seeking to keep his temple the central pillar of Israel's worship while at the same time acknowledging that God can't be localized at any one geographical point.

While it is true that we can pray to God anywhere, it has been the experience of God's people through the generations that our ability to believe and seek God can be enhanced by being in places that have been set aside for prayer.

Question 5. I find that a pattern and a place of prayer are helpful for cycles of time. But after a while I find that I need to change my pattern and place. If I do not change, my times of worship and prayer seem to dry up. Some people find their prayers are enhanced by using a devotional guide such as *My Utmost for His Highest* by Oswald Chambers. Use this question to explore a variety of suggestions from your group.

Question 6. Solomon addresses personal conflicts in verses 31-32, national conflicts in verses 33-35, droughts in verses 35-37 and famine and plagues in verses 37-40. Solomon goes on to address a couple of other areas in verses 41-51.

Question 7. This will vary from person to person. Some people might not think that there is any area they don't pray about. I find that issues that are really personal are difficult for me to bring to God. For instance, in the face of termination of one ministry and the call to another I found it hard to pray. As I puzzled this through I discovered that there were hurts in my past that I had yet to face and bring to God. Use the questions here to help people in your group examine their own patterns of prayer.

Question 8. Solomon is aware that God and Israel are bound together by a covenant. The good news is that God can be appealed to on the basis of His promises. The bad news is that when Israel breaks the terms of the covenant God is justified in bringing punishment. The second good news is that God is forgiving and extends forgiveness when guilt is acknowledged and mercy is requested.

Question 9. Prayer can *create* problems of spiritual intimacy. We must face our own sinfulness at the same time that we come near to God in His holiness. This makes prayer into something of a swing between the poles of attraction and avoidance. It is only as we grow in the knowledge of forgiveness because of Christ's blood that we can enter into the depths and power of Christian prayer.

Question 10. The contemporary charismatic movement has keyed in on this prayer form. This may be an attraction for some and a turnoff for others. The point to keep in mind is that raised hands is a biblical pattern of prayer. When we come to God with our hands open we are setting a posture with our bodies that can be an aid to our hearts as well. We are offering ourselves to God and making ourselves open to receive what God may choose to give.

Question 11. Encourage members of your group to take whatever prayer position they feel comfortable with. See if you can create a sense of permission to pray standing, kneeling, with hands spread, with eyes open or closed — or whatever other way members might desire. Then pray together using the suggestions listed. Interweave silent and spoken prayers.

Study Six
The Prayer of Prevailing Pursuit
Daniel 9:1-19

Purpose: To learn how to prevail in prayer for others by approaching God with boldness and humility.

Question 2. Daniel is intense and serious. He does not assume that because God said He would restore Judah after seventy years that it would automatically happen. He knew that God's will must be prayed into reality.

Question 3. Evidently Daniel was having his quiet time in Jeremiah when he came across the passage telling that God was going to exile Judah for 70 years and then restore it. (See Jeremiah 25:12-14.) This passage illustrates one of the principles of prayer running throughout this guide: prayer is asking God to do what He has promised to do.

Question 4. Fasting, sackcloth, and ashes helped Daniel to enter into his prayer with both body and soul. The Old Testament saints felt that you should not merely pray in your heart or with words, but with your whole being.

Question 5. Your group may provide a variety of explanations here. One possibility is that most Christian churches and fellowships in the Western world are uncomfortable with outward displays of intense inward spiritual realities. The spiritual and religious resistance produced by the Enlightenment and our materialistic culture creates deep and pervasive spiritual inhibitions within us. In addition, we are no longer aware that biblical prayer assumes that God is not merely to be asked in a formal and "proper" way, but beseeched and persuaded with all the intensity that we can muster. Use the second half of the question to explore culturally acceptable ways to worship God with our whole being.

Question 6. Each of Daniel's phrases is worth examining: "we have sinned and done wrong," "we have been wicked and rebelled," "we have turned away from your commands and laws," "we have not listened to your servants the prophets." This final phrase is an acknowledgment that Judah refused to listen to God's warnings for over 200 years. God sent prophet after prophet to tell the people that they were breaking the covenant and would be punished if they didn't repent.

Question 7. Daniel's prayer acknowledges that no area of Jewish society was guiltless; no part of the people in the land could declare their innocence: not the city of Jerusalem, not the province of Judah, not the province of Israel, not the kings, not the common people. As he says in verse 11, "All Israel has transgressed your law."

Question 8. This question can help you explore the broader dimensions of prayer. Whether we are aware of it or not, we come to God as a member of His people. The sins that Daniel was confessing took place seventy years and more in the past, things that were done before he was born. His sense of being a part of the whole nation, however, meant that Daniel felt a part of that history of sin. He did not say, "Forgive my forefathers for they sinned." Instead he said, "We are covered with shame . . . because of our unfaithfulness to you" (verse 7).

As we pray for others we should assume the same posture as Daniel. Rather than asking that *those sinners* be helped, we must say, just as Jesus taught us, "Our Father . . . forgive us our sins."

Daniel never did get back to Jerusalem. His satisfaction would come from the spiritual service and connection he would have with future generations who benefited from his prayers.

You may have to pause and allow your group members time to stretch out their idea of prayer to see how their personal prayers include other people.

Question 9. For background you could read some of the curses and blessings of the covenant given in Deuteronomy 28 and 29. God is doing what He said He would do. He is committed to keeping His end of the covenant and shows Himself faithful to the agreement.

Question 10. This question may come as a shock. Don't allow your group to be put off by it. In the end, discipline by God is preferable to being abandoned by God. The most important blessing is His promise to be our God and to make us His people. When we discover that He won't desert us no matter what we do, we can find strength.

Question 11. Although Daniel's prayer starts with an appeal to the covenant, in his conclusion he appeals to God's history of care and identity with the nation. (Moses did the same after Israel worshiped the golden calf, Exodus 32:11-14.) Your group can point out appropriate phrases in the Daniel text—and comment on them.

Question 12. Although Daniel acknowledges that God caused their defeat and dispersion, he never blames God for Israel's troubles. He acknowledges that their problems were the just result of their sin. Along with that, he presses with all his might to seek God's kindness based on God's honor and His mercy.

For Further Reading

Aharoni, Yohanan, and Michael Avi-Yonah, eds. *The MacMillan Bible Atlas.* Revised Edition. New York and London: Collier MacMillan Publishers, 1977.

Bright, John. *A History of Israel.* 3d ed. Philadelphia: The Westminster Press, 1981.

Chambers, Oswald. *My Utmost for His Highest.* Tarrytown, NY: Fleming H. Revell, 1989.

Douglas, J.D., F.F. Bruce, J.I. Packer, N. Hillyer, D. Guthrie, A.R. Millard, and D.J. Wiseman, eds. *New Bible Dictionary.* 2d ed. Leicester, England: Inter-Varsity, 1982.

Eyre, Stephen. *Drawing Close to God: A LifeGuide Quiet Time Resource.* Downers Grove, Ill.: InterVarsity, 1995.

_____. *Spiritual Disciplines.* (Discipleship Series. Grand Rapids: Zondervan, 1992.

Eyre, Stephen and Jacalyn. *Spiritual Encounter Series.* Downers Grove, Ill.: InterVarsity, 1994.
    Anticipating Christ's Return
    Daring to Follow Jesus
    Enjoying Christ's Blessing
    Entering God's Presence
    Sinking Your Roots into Christ
    Sitting at the Feet of Jesus
    Waiting on the Lord

Fee, Gordon D., and Douglas Stuart. *How to Read the Bible for All It's Worth.* Grand Rapids: Zondervan, 1981.

Ferguson, Sinclair B. and David F. Wright, eds. *New Dictionary of Theology.* Downers Grove, Ill. and Leicester, England: Inter-Varsity, 1988.

Finzel, Hans. *Observe Interpret Apply: How to Study the Bible Inductively.* Wheaton, Ill.: Victor Books, 1994.

Foster, Richard J. *Celebration of Discipline.* San Francisco: HarperCollins, 1978.

_____. *Prayer: Finding the Heart's True Home.* San Francisco: HarperCollins, 1992.

Gorman, Julie A. *Community That is Christian: A Handbook for Small Groups.* Wheaton, Ill.: Victor Books, 1993.

Kuhatschek, Jack. *Taking the Guesswork out of Applying the Bible.* Downers Grove, Ill.: InterVarsity, 1990.

Plueddemann, Jim and Carol. *Pilgrims in Progress: Growing through Groups.* Wheaton, Ill.: Harold Shaw Publishers, 1990.

Swanson, Kenneth. *Uncommon Prayer: Approaching Intimacy with God.* New York: Ballantine Epiphany, 1990.

Tenney, Merrill C., ed. *The Zondervan Pictorial Encyclopedia of the Bible.* 5 vols. Grand Rapids: Zondervan, 1975, 1976.

Walvoord, John F., and Roy B. Zuck, eds. *The Bible Knowledge Commentary, Old Testament.* Wheaton, Ill.: Victor, 1985.

Wenham, G.J., J.A. Motyer, D.A. Carson, and R.T. France, eds. *New Bible Commentary: 21st Century Edition.* Downers Grove, Ill. and Leicester, England: InterVarsity, 1994.

White, John. *Daring to Draw Near: People in Prayer.* Downers Grove, Ill.: InterVarsity. 1977.

Wiseman, D.J., ed. *Tyndale Old Testament Commentaries,* 24. vols. Downers Grove, Ill. and Leicester, England: InterVarsity, 1964–1993.

Wuthnow, Robert, *Sharing the Journey: Support Groups and America's New Quest for Community.* New York: The Free Press, 1994.

About the Author

An ordinary day in Cincinnati will find Stephen Eyre walking his daily route around a lake. An hour to walk and pray (a hobby and a spiritual discipline) is part of his normal routine. Steve became a Christian after his first year of college and has been a determined follower of Jesus Christ ever since. He graduated from Clearwater Christian College with a B.A. degree in History. He went on to earn an M.Div. from Covenant Theological Seminary.  From there Steve spent sixteen years as a staff member of InterVarsity Christian Fellowship helping other college students search out their faith. His work for InterVarsity took him throughout the southeastern section of the United States and eventually to London.

Besides walking, Steve's hobbies include reading and music. He likes to read three books simultaneously: one on theology, one about cultural concerns, and one just for fun. His current "fun" reading is an allegorical fantasy by Guy Guival Kay. Among his book friends, Steve considers C.S. Lewis and Jonathan Edwards his spiritual mentors. As for music, Steve appreciates Georg P. Telemann, a German composer from the 18th century. He also likes *The Cranberries* — thanks to the educational influence of his three teenage sons.

Steve is the author of more than fourteen books and study guides including the *Spiritual Encounter Series* (IVP). He now serves as Associate Pastor for Discipleship at Crestview Presbyterian Church in Cincinnati, Ohio. Steve and his wife Jacalyn have been married for twenty years.